The Complete Guitar Player Classical Book

by Russ Shipton

Exclusive Distributors:
Music Sales Limited
8/9 Frith Street, London W1V 5TZ, England.
Music Sales Pty Limited
120 Rothschild Avenue, Rosebery,
NSW 2018, Australia.
Music Sales Corporation
257 Park Avenue South, New York, NY10010,
United States of America.

Order No. AM38217
ISBN 0-7119-0592-4
This book © Copyright 1985, 1995 by
Wise Publications

Art direction by Mike Bell
Designed by Alison Fenton
Cover photography by Peter Wood

Your Guarantee of Quality
As publishers, we strive to produce every
book to the highest commercial standards.
Throughout, the printing and binding have been
planned to ensure a sturdy, attractive publication
which should give years of enjoyment.
If your copy fails to meet our high standards,
please inform us and we will gladly replace it.

Music Sales' complete catalogue describes thousands
of titles and is available in full colour sections by subject,
direct from Music Sales Limited. Please state your areas of interest
and send a cheque/postal order for £1.50 for postage to:
Music Sales Limited, Newmarket Road, Bury St. Edmunds,
Suffolk IP33 3YB.

Printed in the United Kingdom by
Halstan & Co Limited, Amersham, Buckinghamshire.

Wise Publications
London/New York/Paris/Sydney/Copenhagen/Madrid

Contents

Music in this book

Alternate Melody (Shipton)
Allegretto (Giuliani)
Maestoso (Giuliani)
Andantino (Sor)
Moderato (Sor)
Hungarian Air (Bathioli)
Waltz I (Carcassi)
A Minor Melody (Shipton)
Waltz (Carulli)
Allegretto (Giuliani)
Study (Diabelli)
Allegro in C (Sor)
Waltz II (Carcassi)
In Tandem (Shipton)
Prelude (Aguado)
Study (Sor)
Dance (Giuliani)
March (Clarke)
Theme & Variation (Carulli)
Study (Giuliani)
Ecossaise (Anon.)
Off & On (Shipton)
Moderato in D (Diabelli)
Moderato (Sor)
Open Air (Shipton)
Pavanes I & II (Milan)
Common Triplets (Shipton)
Study (Giuliani)
Village Waltz (Shipton)
Bush Jig (Shipton)
The Duke's March (Shipton)
Minuet in F (Diabelli)
Bourrée (De Visée)
Minuet (J. S. Bach)
Greensleeves (Anon.)
Spanish Ballad, Romanza (Anon.)
Bourrée (J. S. Bach)
Scarborough Fair (Trad.)

The Classical Playing Position

The Right-Hand Position

It is very important for the right hand to have both freedom and economy of movement. Thus, the wrist should arc **slightly,** and the hand should be at right angles to the strings.

It is vital that the muscles be relaxed, not tight. The thumb should be held a little to the left of the fingers so both thumb and fingers have unrestricted movement. The thumb is generally held over the three bass strings, while the fingers cover the treble strings.

In the classical position, the guitar rests on the left leg, which is raised a little by a small stool (or an alternative). This position allows maximum freedom of movement for the hands without causing discomfort for the body as a whole.

The right arm rests on the top right of the guitar body, with the right hand positioned approximately over the sound hole. Keep your back straight, with the neck of the guitar at a 45° angle – try to imitate the position shown, remembering that it is very important to feel relaxed and comfortable.

The left arm is held reasonably close (but not tight) to the body. The thumb rests about midway on the back of the neck, and supports the pressure of the left-hand fingers.

Right-Hand Finger Indications

The right-hand fingering is indicated by the letters *p, i, m* and *a* (from the Spanish terminology). These letters are shown above the stave:

p = the right-hand thumb

i = the index finger

m = the middle finger

a = the third or ring finger

The little finger on the right hand is not used.

Nails

The thumbnail should be grown reasonably long for the thumb-strokes to be effective in the position shown. The fingernails need be only a little longer than the tips of the fingers.

The Left-Hand Position

Hold your arm a few inches from your body so that the left arm and hand are roughly in line and at right angles to the neck of the guitar. The left hand fingers will then have both freedom and economy of movement.

The thumb should be placed midway on the back of the neck, providing a firm grip with the fingers on the strings. The wrist should not be pushed too far forward, otherwise the grip is lost and the muscles strained. The palm of the hand and front of the fingers should be kept clear of the neck.

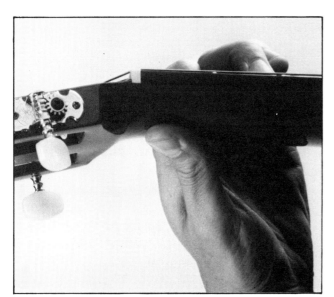

In order to obtain clarity of sound, the tips of the left-hand fingers must come down **firmly** on the strings, as close to the fretwire in front of them as possible. This will avoid both buzzing noises and the necessity to press down too hard.

For the music in the first half of the book, your left hand fingers will be in what is known as 'first position'. This means that each finger is generally expected to press down notes on its appropriate fret, i.e. the first finger presses down notes on the first fret, the second finger those on the second fret, and so on.

Left-Hand Finger Indications

The suggested left-hand fingering is usually placed next to the notes on the treble clef. The fingers are represented by numbers:

1 = the index finger

2 = the middle finger

3 = the ring finger

4 = the little finger

The left-hand thumb is not used in classical playing.

Nails

The nails of the left-hand fingers should be kept very short. Nails that aren't short will prevent the fingertip providing enough pressure on the string to produce a clear note.

Here are the open-string notes for the guitar, written in the treble clef. The appropriate strings are indicated below on a 'window' of the guitar fingerboard. Memorize these notes:

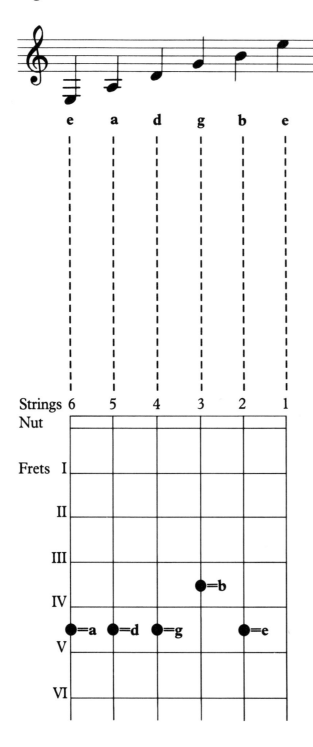

The dots shown on the window diagram are the positions on the fingerboard that will produce the same notes as the adjacent open strings.

Relative Tuning

The easiest way to tune your guitar is to find a reference point for the lowest string (E), and then to tune the other strings to it by means of 'relative tuning'. There are various ways of finding the low E, but by far the easiest is to use a tuning fork or pitch pipes. Most guitarists use the relative tuning method, which is explained below:

1 Tighten the 1st string to the correct pitch (approximate if a tuning device is not available).

2 Tighten the 2nd string until the note on the 5th fret is equal in pitch to the open 1st string.

3 Tighten the 3rd string until the note on the 4th fret is equal in pitch to the open 2nd string.

4 Tighten the 4th string until the note on the 5th fret is equal in pitch to the open 3rd string.

5 Tighten the 5th string until the note on the 5th fret is equal in pitch to the open 4th string.

6 Tighten the 6th string until the note on the 5th fret is equal in pitch to the open 5th string.

Then you should check through again, in case any of the strings have noticeably loosened, as they are inclined to do when first used.

Reading Music

Books 2 and 3 of **The Complete Guitar Player** have the details of the music theory you need to know for the pieces in this book. A summary of this information is shown on the pull-out card.

Should you want more information, I recommend **How To Read Music** by Helen Cooper, published by Omnibus Press (a division of Music Sales Limited), Order No. OP41904 (Book only); AM91452 (Book and CD).

Tirando (free stroke)

Most notes are struck with a free stroke or tirando, and to begin with all the pieces in this book should be played using *only* free strokes. The finger strikes the string while bent, and comes to rest in the air above the string, not on another string. Generally the string is struck first by the flesh of the fingertip, followed immediately by the nail. Using the 1st finger and a free stroke, strike the first string. Then try a free stroke with the thumb on the sixth string.

Thumb strikes   After striking

Alternating Right-Hand Fingers

An important rule in classical guitar playing is the alternation of fingers when the same string is played consecutively. The third example below involves this right-hand technique. Follow the finger indications carefully.

Finger strikes   After striking

Open-string Exercises

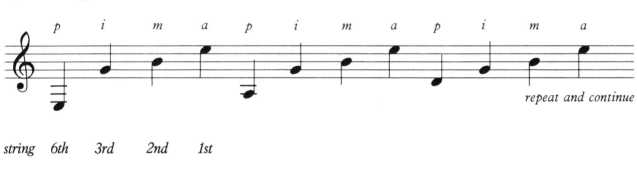

Alternate Melody Russ Shipton

This simple piece involves minims and crotchets only. A **minim** (𝅗𝅥) lasts for two beats, and a **crotchet** (♩) one.

The **time signature** of ₄² means that each bar has two beats, and each beat is one crotchet in duration.

Count an even **1**, 2 for each bar, as shown beneath the stave.

The 'o' next to a note indicates that the open string is played.

The :‖ sign means play that section again.

Moderato means that the piece should be played at a moderate speed, but as with all the pieces in this book, play this one slowly at first.

Left-Hand Positions

Bar 1 (**c** note)

Bar 3 (**d** note)

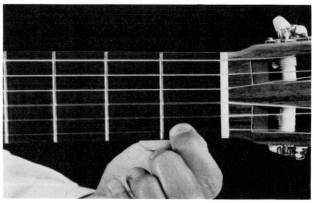

Bar 5 (**f** note)

Play this piece and the others in the book with **free strokes only**. After reaching the rest-stroke information on page 55, you can go through all the pieces again and use the rest stroke where you feel it may add to the interpretation of the piece.

Allegretto Mauro Giuliani

Giuliani was born in Bologna, Italy, in 1781 and died in Vienna in 1829. He was a very popular composer throughout Europe, and many of his simpler pieces are used for teaching the guitar today.

Here is another simple piece with crotchets and minims. The right-hand fingering includes the ring finger this time, in the fifth bar.

Stress the first beat of each bar slightly more than the second.

Be sure to allow each note its full value by not removing your left-hand finger, until the moment you strike the next string.

Allegretto is Italian for moderately fast.

Left-Hand Positions

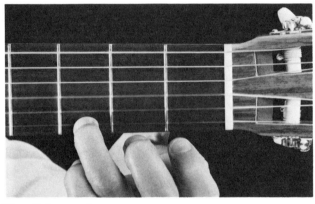

Bar 2 (**g** note)

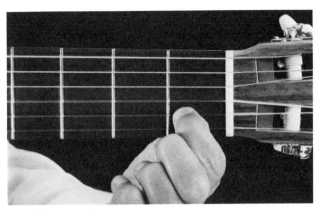

Bar 5 (**c** note)

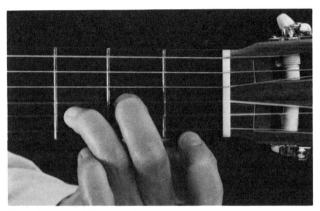

Bar 6 (**a** and **d** notes)

Allegretto

Maestoso Mauro Giuliani

Both **semibreves** (○) and crotchets are used in this second Giuliani piece, which is written in the time signature of $\frac{4}{4}$. This means there are four beats in each bar, and as in $\frac{2}{4}$, each beat is one crotchet in duration.

Stress the first beat of each bar a little more than the others, and count the beats as shown below the stave.

All the notes in this arrangement are played by the right-hand thumb.

D.C. (da capo) al Fine means return to the beginning of the piece and play until you reach the word **Fine.**

Maestoso is an Italian word meaning majestically. That's how this piece should be played!

Left-Hand Positions

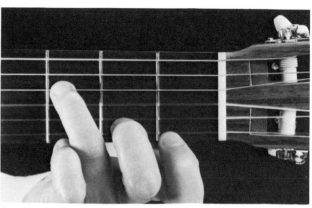

Bar 2 (**f** note)

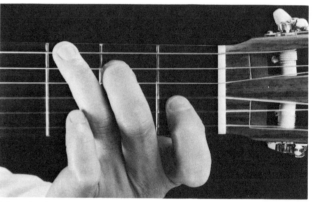

Bar 3 (**b** and **g** notes)

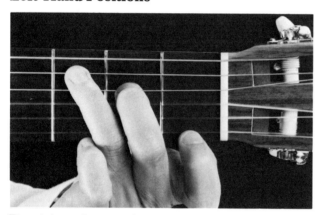

Bar 1 (**e** and **c** notes)

Maestoso

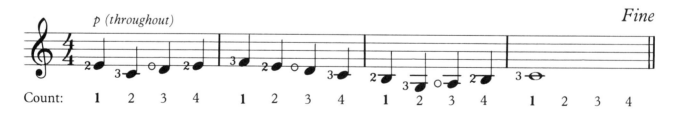

Andantino Fernando Sor

Watch for the only thumb strike of the piece in the fourth bar.

Sometimes the right-hand fingers must cross over – for example, when going from the **c** to the **e** in the first bar. The 3rd finger may sometimes be used to avoid this, but whatever fingers are used, alternating them is necessary for smooth playing.

Andantino means fairly slow, although a little faster than **andante.**

Left-Hand Positions

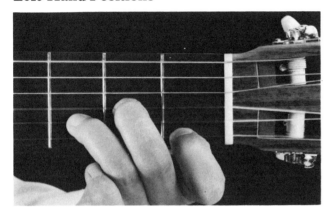

Bar 3 (**a, f** and **d** notes)

Bar 4 (**f** note)

Andantino

Moderato Fernando Sor

Fernando Sor was born in 1778 and died in 1839. A Spaniard who moved to France, he became famous throughout Europe for his compositions and concert playing.

Sor was also the first guitarist to popularize the instrument in Britain in the early 19th century. He is, perhaps, the most influential of all the early classical guitar composers and players.

The second piece from Sor has a $\frac{3}{4}$ time signature. This means there are three beats to each bar and, once again, each beat is a crotchet's duration. Stress the first beat of each bar and think of a waltz rhythm.

The last bar has a **dotted minim** (♩.). A dot **after** a note means that it lasts half as long again. Thus, the dotted minim is the same length as three crotchets.

Quavers (♫) are included in this piece. Two are played in the time of one crotchet. Count them as shown beneath the stave.

Left-Hand Positions

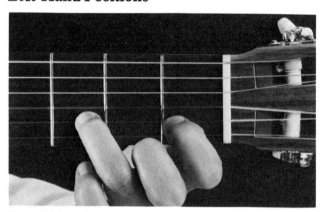

Bar 4 (d to **c)**

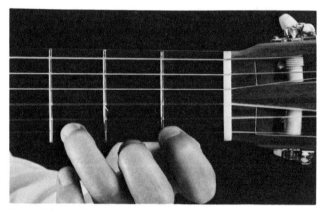

Bar 6 (g to **f)**

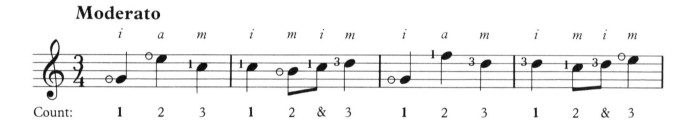

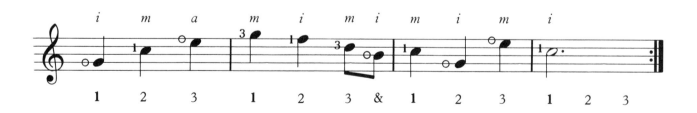

Hungarian Air Bathioli

The arrangement of this 19th century piece includes thumb strikes on just the fourth string **e** notes.

You'll notice that the **g** notes are altered by the **sharp sign** (♯) shown next to them. This sharp sign raises the note by one semitone (fret). Instead of playing the open third string, play the **g♯** note on the first fret of the third string.

When a note is altered by a sign shown immediately before it, this sign is called an **accidental.** An explanation of accidentals can be found later in the book when the concept of keys is discussed.

Play this piece at a moderate speed and try, as you always should, to give every note its full value.

Left-Hand Positions

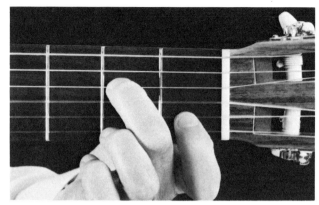

Bar 2 (**e** note)

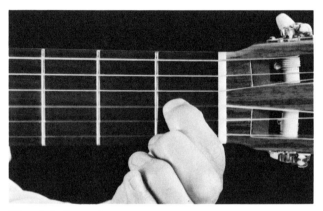

Bar 4 (**g**♯ note)

Moderato

Waltz I Matteo Carcassi

Matteo Carcassi was born in 1792 and came from Italy to Paris with a reputation as a fine concert player. He became well-known in Europe after the publication of many of his pieces. He died in 1853.

Here, the right hand must play more than one string at the same time. This involves a pinching action by the thumb and finger, plucking notes up and down at the same time. (The technique is widely used in folk picking, and is described and illustrated in Books 2 and 3 of **The Complete Guitar Player**).

In bars 3 and 4, two right-hand fingers pluck at the same time – this is also used in traditional, as well as classical music.

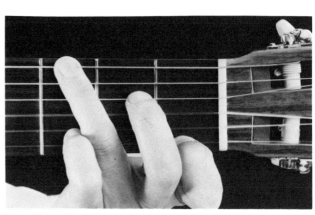

Bar 3 (**g** and **f** notes)

Left-Hand Positions

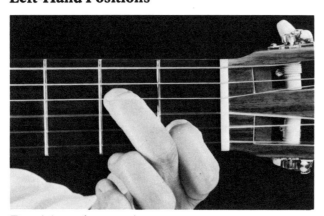

Bar 1 (**e** and **c** notes)

Andantino

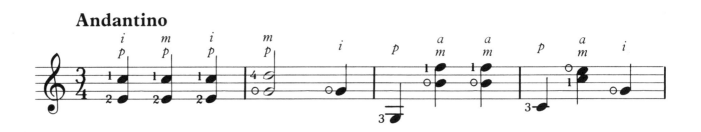

A Minor Melody Russ Shipton

Here, quavers are grouped in fours. This is done for easier reading.

The accidental sign applies throughout the same bar. Thus the second **g** is played sharp in the 4th and 7th bars.

The **Fermata** sign (⌒) above the last note means that the note is allowed to ring on longer than written. Often the fermata is used in the middle of a piece as a 'meaningful pause'.

Left-Hand Positions

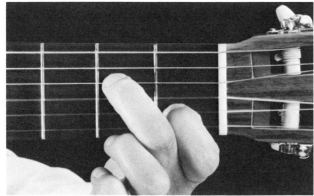

Bar 1 (Keep the 1st finger on the **c** note for the first 3½ bars).

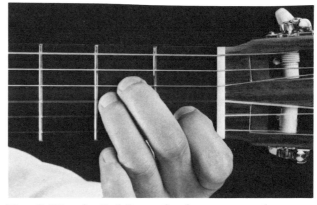

Bar 3 (Use the 3rd finger for the **a** note at the start of bar 3).

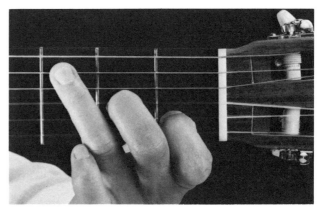

Bar 5 (In this and other bars, leave fingers on where the same notes are repeated).

Moderato

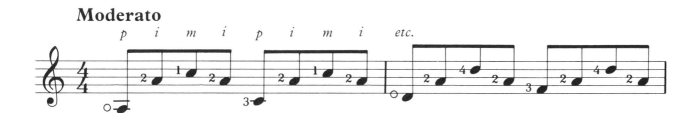

15

In order that guitar music can be read more easily, it is usually split into two parts: bass and treble. Each part must add up to the appropriate time value per bar, according to the time signature involved.

Waltz Ferdinando Carulli

Ferdinando Carulli (1770–1841) was largely a self-taught guitarist who settled in Paris and became well-known as a teacher and performer. His compositions were generally simpler than Sor's or Carcassi's, but all three shared a strong melodic feel.

This piece has a time signature of $\frac{3}{4}$, so each part should be equal to the length of three crotchets per bar.

Learn each part separately, and then put them together, bar by bar.

The top line is the melody – emphasize this a little more than the bass line.

Don't forget the repeat!

Left-Hand Positions

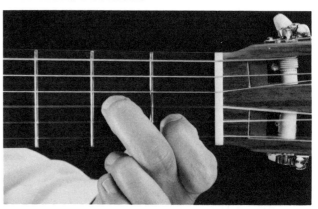

Bar 1 (hold **a** and **c** notes for the first two bars)

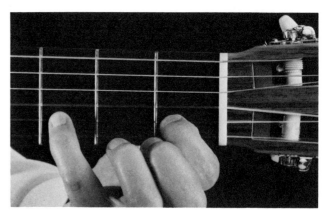

Bar 7 (**d** to **c**)

Moderato

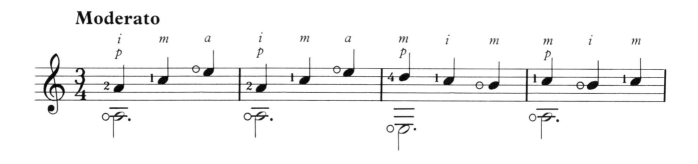

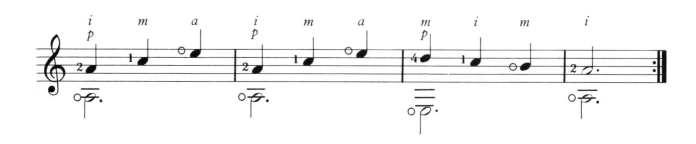

Allegretto Mauro Giuliani

This piece was shown on page 9, but here a bass part has been added.

Notice that, when writing guitar music in two parts, the stems of the treble notes point upwards while the stems of the bass notes point downwards.

Generally, the treble part is the melody, and is played by the right-hand fingers, while the bass is the harmony, played by the right-hand thumb.

Notice the use of the fourth finger now that a bass part has been included.

Allegretto means moderately fast.

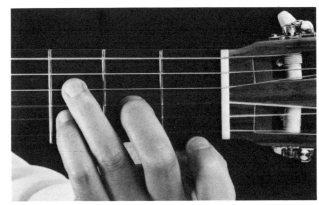

Bar 6 (**f**, **a** and **d** notes)

Left-Hand Positions

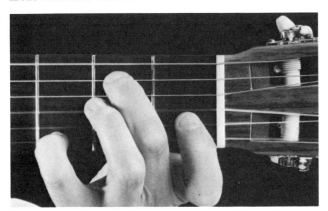

Bar 2 (**b** and **g** notes)

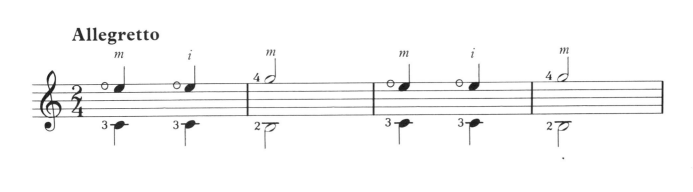

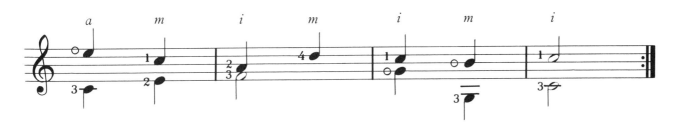

Study Anton Diabelli

Anton Diabelli, (1781-1853), went to Vienna from his native Italy, and taught both piano and guitar. In 1818, he formed a publishing partnership and subsequently became Schubert's publisher. (He is also the Diabelli of Beethoven's famous variations).

This piece includes crotchet and quaver rests. Work out the relationship of the timing between the two parts for each bar. Check the counts shown below the stave.

Additional harmony notes may be included in the treble part when they are to be played by the right-hand fingers. Their stems are joined together.

Try to space the notes on the beats as evenly as possible, otherwise your playing will sound jerky and you won't do justice to the piece.

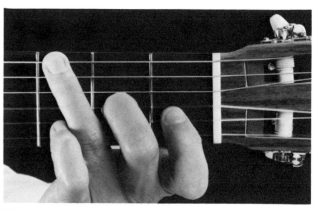

Bar 3 (finger **g**, then **a** note)

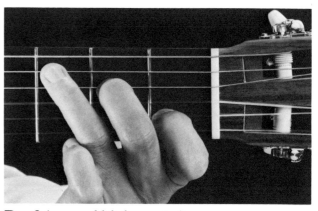

Bar 8 (**c, e** and **high c** notes)

Left-Hand Positions

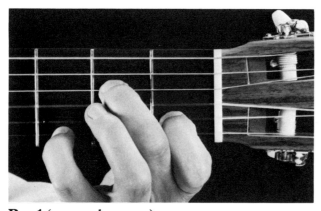

Bar 1 (**e, c** and **g** notes)

Allegro in C Fernando Sor

Both crotchet and minim rests occur in this piece by Sor. Check the timing of the 1st bar carefully – though the first treble note lasts for two beats, the first bass note is played on the second beat. Use the count below the stave to help you.

When similar bars are repeated, use the same fingering as before.

Notice that the third string is struck by the right-hand fingers when in the treble part, and by the thumb when in the bass part.

Allegro means fast and lively, so when you've mastered the timing and fingering, increase the tempo – gradually.

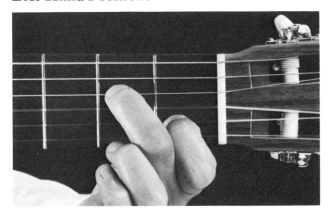

Bar 4 (**a** and **f** notes)

Left-Hand Positions

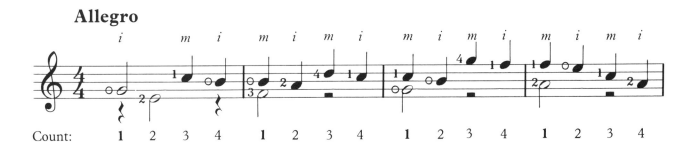

Bar 1 (**e** and **c** notes)

The C Major Scale

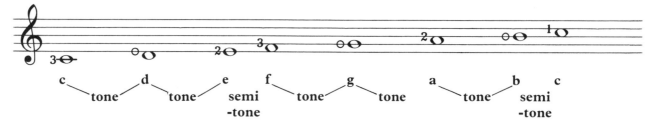

c — tone — d — tone — e — semi-tone — f — tone — g — tone — a — tone — b — semi-tone — c

Some of the pieces you've seen so far have ended with a **c** note. These (and most other pieces ending with a **c** note) are said to be in the key of C. This means that the melody 'revolves' around the **c** note, and the other notes expected to occur in the melody are those in the scale of **C Major.** Use the left-hand fingering shown, and play the scale with alternating index and middle fingers of the right hand.

All major scales share a common interval structure, i.e. **tone, tone, semitone, tone, tone, tone, semitone.**

Have a look at the first five pieces in the book, and you'll see that all the notes come from the C major scale. In this scale, there are no sharp or flat notes.

Left-Hand Positions

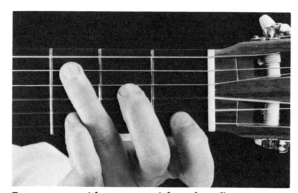

Low c note (then open 4th string **d**)

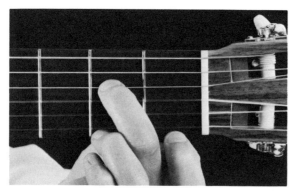

e note

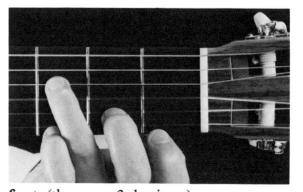

f note (then open 3rd string **g**)

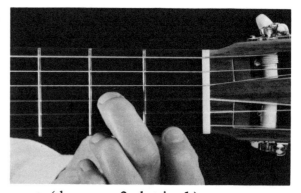

a note (then open 2nd string **b**)

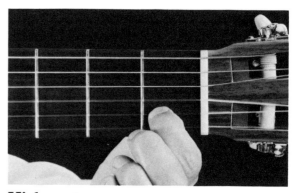

High c note

Waltz II Matteo Carcassi

Other major scales, beginning with different notes, will need sharp or flat notes to maintain the correct major scale interval structure. The second Carcassi Waltz, below, is in the key of C, but for one bar, (the 7th), it passes through the key of G major, which we'll examine on the following page. With a temporary key change such as this one, an 'accidental' sharp or flat sign is used next to the note that is to be altered. In this case the **f** notes in the 7th bar (but **only** that bar) are made sharp.

Often treble and bass parts divide neatly, but sometimes notes can be considered as either melody or accompaniment. For ease of reading, notes may be included in both treble and bass parts, and have downward as well as upward stems. The first note of most bars in this piece are counted as quavers in the treble part, and dotted minims in the bass.

Notice the lead-in note before the first full bar. The last bar of the piece has just two beats to take account of this lead-in note.

Left-Hand Positions

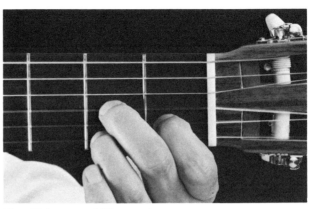

Bar 7 (**a, c** and **f**♯ notes)

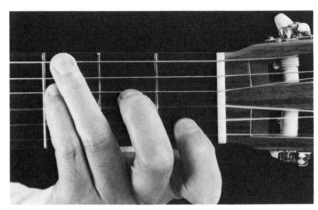

Bar 15 (**g** and **f** notes)

21

The G Major Scale:

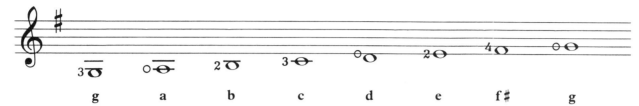

g   a   b   c   d   e   f♯   g

Like the key of C major, the key of **G major** is one of several keys favoured by guitarists because simpler fingering is entailed. When a piece is written in G major, the notes expected to occur in the melody will be those notes forming the G major scale:

g   a   b   c   d   e   f♯   g

In order to maintain the correct major scale intervals between notes, the **f** note must be made sharp. Play the G major scale and compare it to the C major scale.

Key signatures

When a piece is written in the key of G major, to save writing a sharp sign next to all **f** notes, and to clarify the key of the piece, a **key signature** is used. In the case of G major, a sharp sign is placed on the **f** line of the stave. This means that *all* **f** notes, whatever the octave, must be made sharp.

Octaves

A note of the same name appears in each octave. Find and play the scale of G major one octave higher than the one shown. It begins with the open third string and ends with the **g** note on 3rd fret, first string.

Left-Hand Positions

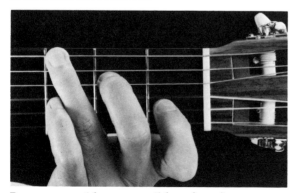

Low g note (then open 5th string **a**)

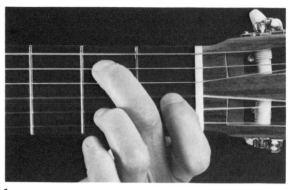

b note

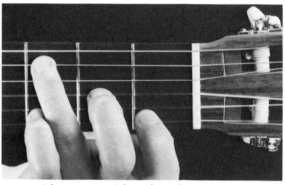

c note (then open 4th string **d**)

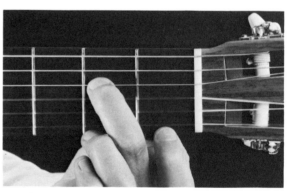

e note

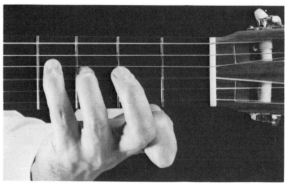

f♯ note (then 3rd string **g**)

In Tandem Russ Shipton

Notice that each line of music begins with the key signature, whereas the time signature is written only at the start of the piece.

The $\frac{4}{4}$ rhythm often used to be referred to as **common time**. You may sometimes see a large **C** instead of $\frac{4}{4}$, as shown below.

Remember to play **f♯** notes in bars 3, 4 and 7.

Left-Hand Positions

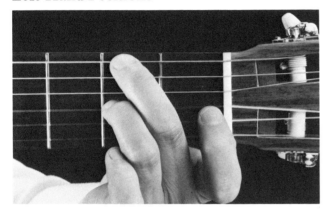

Bar 3 (**f♯** and **a** notes)

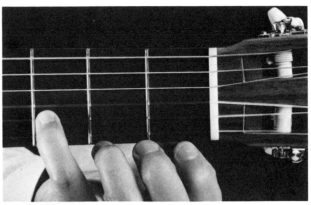

Bar 7 (**d** note)

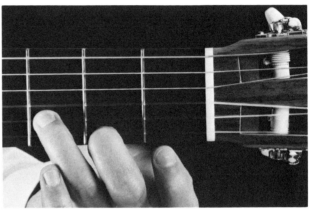

Bar 7 (**f♯** and **d** notes)

Andantino

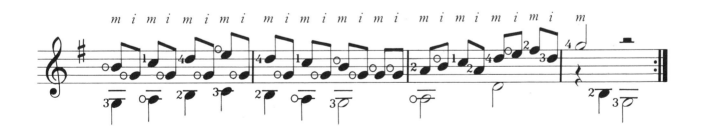

23

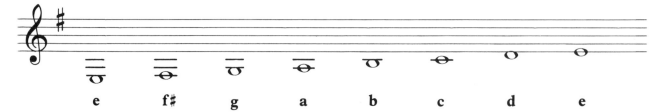

The E Minor Scale

| e | f♯ | g | a | b | c | d | e |

The major scale has been a cornerstone of Western music for several centuries. The other important scale to form a basis for composition is the minor scale. This scale has several slightly differing forms, but each minor scale is related to the major scale beginning on the note three semitones above it.

g note

The piece by Aguado on the following page is written in the key of **E minor,** which is related to G major (examined on page 22). The same key signature is used for the major and its relative minor key, so E minor has one sharp – f sharp – as well.

The seventh note of a minor scale (before the tonic) is often sharpened but this alteration is made to individual notes and not included in the key signature. In the Prelude on the opposite page, the d notes are sharpened. And you've already seen the **g♯** notes in three previous pieces. The **g** note is the seventh note of the **A minor** scale, and is often made sharp. Play the major and relative minor scales below:

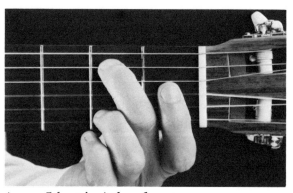

(open 5th string) then **b** note

g a b c d e f♯ g

e f♯ g a b c d e

Left-Hand Positions

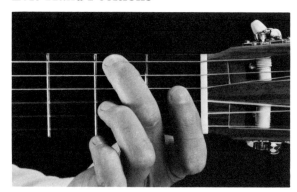

e note (then **f♯**)

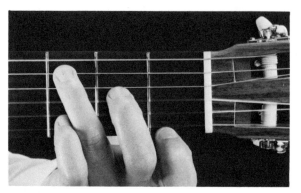

c note

(open 4th string) then **e** note

Minor Keys

Prelude Dionisio Aguado

Dionisio Aguado was born in Madrid in 1784, and after establishing himself in Spain he visited Paris and became friends with Sor. He returned to Spain in 1838, and died there in 1849.

Notice the use of three right-hand fingers in bars 1 and 2, then the use of just index and middle fingers in bars 3 and 4.

The 2nd finger of the left hand remains on the 2nd fret of the 4th string through bars 1 and 2. In bar 3 the 1st and 3rd fingers stay in position while the 4th finger is added. In this way, you can produce a smooth and flowing sound.

So far you've played pieces in three different simple rhythms – $\frac{2}{4}$, $\frac{3}{4}$ and $\frac{4}{4}$. Several other time signatures are used in classical music, the most common is probably $\frac{6}{8}$. The 6 means there are six beats to every bar, and the 8 means that each beat has a time value of one quaver (instead of a crotchet, as in $\frac{2}{4}$, $\frac{3}{4}$ and $\frac{4}{4}$). Thus, each bar would have a total time value of six quavers. Although this adds up to the same **value** as in $\frac{3}{4}$, the **stresses** are different. In $\frac{6}{8}$, each bar normally has a **123, 456** feel, i.e. the first beat carries the main stress, and a subsidiary stress is put on the fourth beat.

Study Fernando Sor

This Study in $\frac{6}{8}$ by Sor involves two main rhythmic patterns: The first is crotchet quaver, crotchet quaver, the second is two groups of three quavers. Both groupings are very characteristic of $\frac{6}{8}$. The bass patterns are a little more varied, so count each bar (and part) separately before playing – the beat count is given below the stave for guidance.

Notice that the dotted crotchet has a time value of one and a half crotchets i.e. three quavers.

For those notes without right or left hand fingering indications, follow the fingering shown for similar positions. Also, watch out for the sharps in the 7th bar.

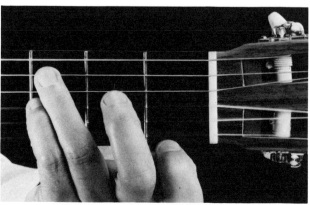

Bar 7 (**c** and **a**♯)

Left-Hand Positions

Bar 1 (**d**♯ and **f**♯ to **e** and **g**)

Moderato

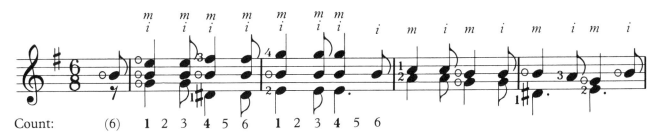

Count: (6) **1** 2 3 **4** 5 6   **1** 2 3 **4** 5 6

1 2 3 **4** 5 6

1 2 3 **4** 5 6

1 2 3 **4** 5 6   **1** 2 3 **4** 5 6

1 2 3 **4** 5 6   **1** 2 3 **4** 5

There is a very important left-hand technique known as a **barré.** This refers to a left-hand finger pressing down more than one string at the same time. The **grand barré** involves the first finger covering all six strings, while the **half** or **small-barré** involves a left-hand finger (normally the 1st) pressing down two to five strings.

Try this half barré shown below:

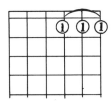

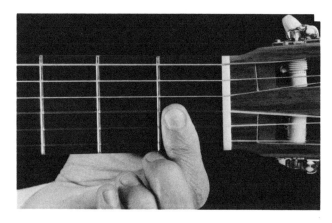

Press all three strings down firmly and then play them individually with your right hand, listening for clarity of sound in each case. Adjust your thumb

on the back of the neck if you're not getting enough pressure. Normally the thumb should be a little lower for barré positions.

Now try the full barré. Place your first finger over all the strings at the first fret, and play the strings individually, again checking for buzz. On many occasions you'll be playing only two or three of the strings barréd by the first finger. Here's the position for the 7th and 15th bars below, where you must play the first, second and sixth strings. These are, therefore, the strings to press down firmly.

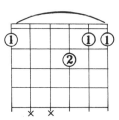

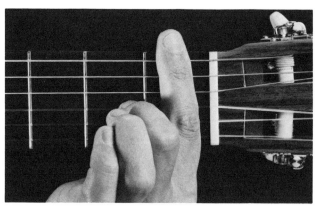

Dance Mauro Giuliani

Giuliani has written many beautiful pieces using the $\frac{6}{8}$ rhythm. I have chosen one dance from a group of four to illustrate the use of the barré and also the **natural** sign (♮). A note may be made sharp or flat by the key signature or by a previous sign in the same bar. A natural sign can reverse this – in the opening run, for example, the accidental **f♯** is followed by a naturalized **f.**

CI means a full barré at the 1st fret.

Left-Hand Positions

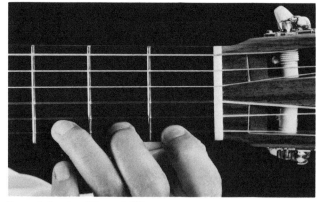

Lead-in (**g, f♯** and **f♮**)

Bar 2 (**c**, **e** and **top c**) then add **d** note   **Bar 7** (**full barré**, then add 4th finger)

Allegretto

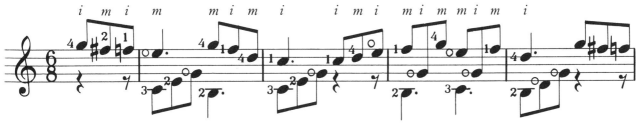

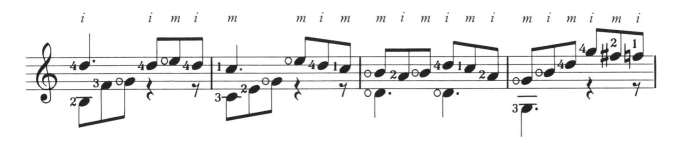

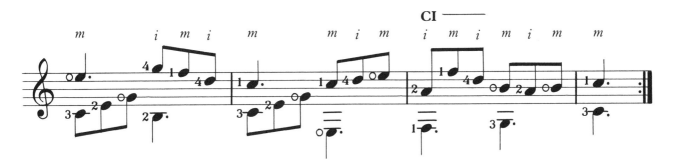

The D Major Scale

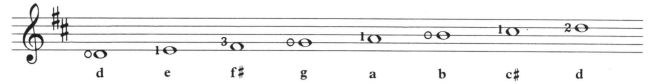

d   e   f♯   g   a   b   c♯   d

The key of D major is another popular key for guitarists. The notes in the D major scale include f♯ (like the G major scale) plus c♯ :

d   e   f♯   g   a   b   c♯   d

The relative minor key of D major is B minor, which entails difficult positions. Consequently, it's rarely encountered in guitar music.

In the piece that follows, and any others in the key of D major, the left hand fingers must be in the '2nd position.' In other words, the 1st finger normally plays notes on the 2nd fret, the 2nd finger plays notes on the 3rd fret, and so on.

Left-Hand Positions

2nd Position

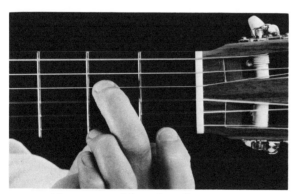

e note (then open 4th string **d**)

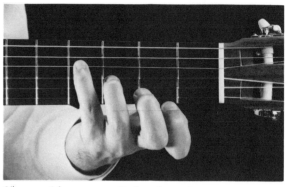

f♯ note (then open 3rd string **g**)

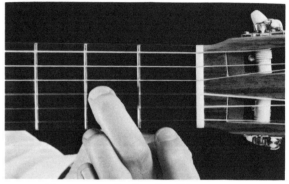

a note (then open 2nd string **b**)

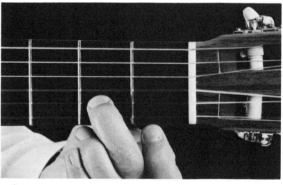

c♯ note

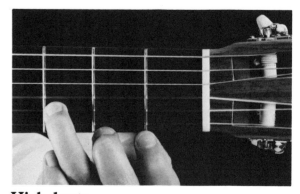

High d note

March Jeremiah Clarke

Jeremiah Clarke (c.1659–1707) was an English composer and organist. Most of his music was for the Church or the stage, though he also wrote a good deal of harpsichord music (from which this piece is probably adapted).

This piece includes an **a** note at the 5th fret on the first string, and you'll need to hold your left hand fingers in the second position, i.e. the 1st finger over the 2nd fret, the 2nd over the 3rd fret and so on. The indicated fingering makes this clear.

Watch out for the dotted crotchets in bars 8 and 16 – the e note is held for one-and-a-half beats, and then the d note is played on the half beat. Count the beats as shown beneath the bar.

A march should be played with a heavier stress than usual on each beat.

31

The $\frac{3}{8}$ rhythm has just one stress in each bar, and that is on the first beat. The **3** of the time signature means that there are three beats to each bar, and the **8** indicates that each beat is a quaver's time value.

The $\frac{3}{8}$ rhythm is normally played crisply and quickly. However, always follow the directions of the composer.

Theme and Variation Ferdinando Carulli

Just one of Carulli's two variations on a theme is given below. In the Variation, one of the changes is the use of semi-quavers (♫). Follow the count given and you'll have no trouble with the rhythm.

Sometimes a bracketed natural sign is placed next to a note to confirm that the accidental in the previous bar doesn't apply, (as in the last bar of the theme below.)

Left-Hand Positions

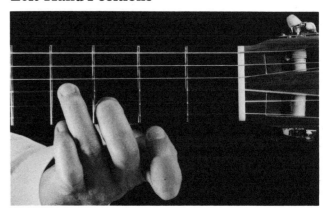

Bar 10 (**b** and **d** notes)

Theme

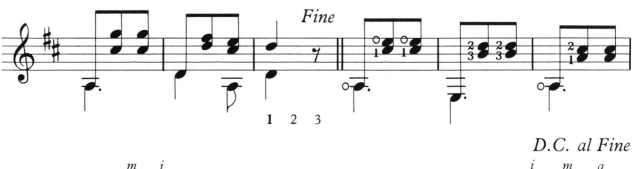

Variation

Count: **1** & 2 & 3 &

Fine

1 & 2 3

D.C. al Fine

p   i   m   i   m   a

The effect of a **drone** can be got by playing the same string continuously with alternating right hand fingers. This technique – the **tremolo** – is very difficult to sustain for some time, particularly when using the third right hand finger as well as the index and middle.

The small tremolo in the piece opposite should be quite easy for you to manage; hold the right hand so the fingers are very close to the strings. Listen carefully to ensure that you are producing a smooth sound – rhythmically and tonally.

Study Mauro Giuliani

This piece in ⅜ is a little different from the previous one – the thumb must play some second and third string notes, and the drone or tremolo is introduced in the second half.

The left-hand fingering is generally straightforward, but those bars which may cause difficulty are marked.

Try to make all the notes of both parts ring out – the harmony lines are certainly worth hearing.

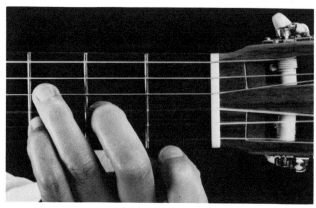

Bar 23 (**f, a** and **d** notes)

Left-Hand Positions

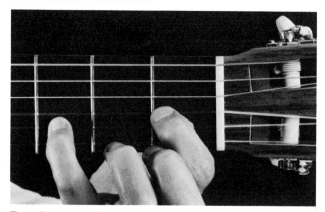

Bar 13 (**g♯** and **d** notes)

Moderato

Fine

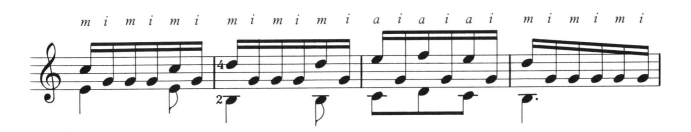

D.C. al Fine

The A Major Scale

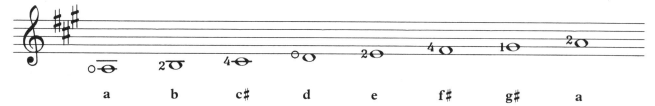

a   b   c#   d   e   f#   g#   a

Another key favoured by guitarists is A major. This scale has three sharps:

a   b   c#   d   e   f#   g#   a

The relative minor scale of A major, which has the same key signature of three sharps, is found three semitones below: F# minor. This minor key is not encountered much because fingering is more difficult.

Music written in the key of A major, like D major, will often involve left-hand fingering in the 2nd position.

Left-Hand Positions

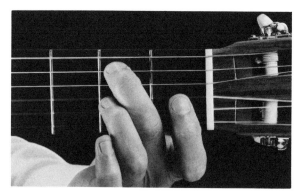

(Open 5th string **a** then) **b** note

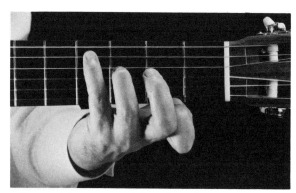

c# note (then open 4th string **d**)

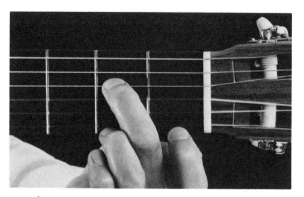

e note

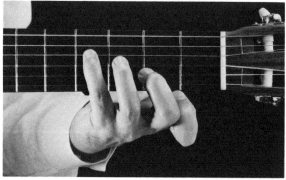

f# note

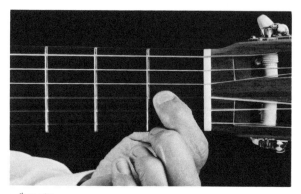

g# note

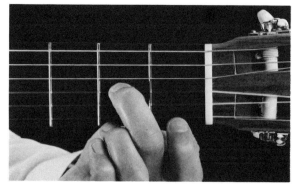

High **a** note

Ecossaise Anon. (c. 1830)

Like the key of D major, melodies in the key of A major usually involve the 2nd position for the left hand fingers. Because of the **g♯** note, however, the left hand must move between the 1st and 2nd positions. The fingering indications will help you with the changes.

Notice that the **b** notes at the start of the 3rd and 7th bars are fingered at the 4th fret, third string.

In the 3rd bar, slide the 2nd finger from the **d** note to the **c♯**, and the 1st finger from the **a** to the **g♯** – with such anchor fingers, the left hand moves become much easier and more accurate.

Notice the accidental **d♯** which applies also to the second **d** note in the third bar of the second section. The natural sign next to the **f** three bars later, cancels the **f♯** in the key signature. The sharp sign then restores it.

In the 1st & 2nd bars of the second section, a device known as a **tie** is used. Rather than write a dotted crotchet, a tie joining crotchet and quaver makes reading the two parts together much easier. Thus, the first **a** note only is played and then held over. Ties are used in several other circumstances which you'll come to later.

Andantino

A curved line, like the tie that you've just seen, but which joins two notes of *different* pitch, means that the **ligado** technique must be used. This involves the left hand creating a second note after the right hand has struck the first. Play the open first string and then hammer-on the 1st fret with your 1st finger – come down firmly behind the fret wire and you should produce a clear second note.

Off & On Russ Shipton

In this piece, every ligado involves an open string. For the descending ligado, you must pull the string slightly (with the left hand) and then let go – this will produce a note of sufficient volume. The last bar has three notes joined by curved lines – the 2nd finger must hammer-on and then pull-off to produce two more notes.

Don't forget the sharp notes, **f#**, **c#**, and **g#**!

Moderato in D Antonio Diabelli

Diabelli's second piece will give you some practice with fretted note ligados. As before, the left hand finger must be poised ready to hammer-on for the ascending ligado, but the finger fretting the second note for a descending ligado must be in place before the right hand strikes the first note.

Left-Hand Positions

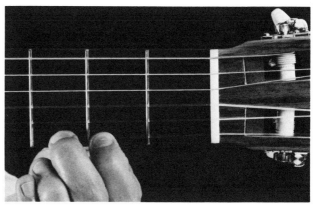

Bar 1 (**g** ligado to **f**♯)

$\frac{2}{2}$ or Cut Time

Previously, we have seen that the symbol, C, may be used instead of the $\frac{4}{4}$ time signature. You will often come across the sign, ₵, which stands for $\frac{2}{2}$ time (commonly referred to as **cut time**). We will discuss $\frac{2}{2}$ in more detail later but, for now, count it as you would $\frac{4}{4}$ and place a little extra stress on beats one and three.

Moderato Fernando Sor

As usual, the bass notes with downward stems are to be played by the right hand thumb. Experiment with your own choice of right hand fingering, but remember that alternating fingers will generally mean smoother playing.

This piece introduces a new sign – the flat (♭), which lowers a note by one semitone (fret).

Notice the b flat (♭) in the 12th bar; also the f♯ in the 14th bar. The left hand fingering is straightforward, and the accidentals create a more interesting harmony with a little more tension.

In the 7th bar the f and g notes are not written in exact vertical line, but they are still played together.

Left-Hand Positions

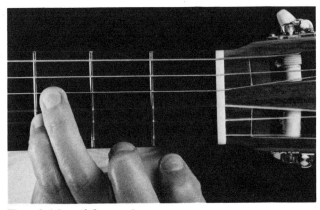

Bar 6 (**d** and **f** notes)

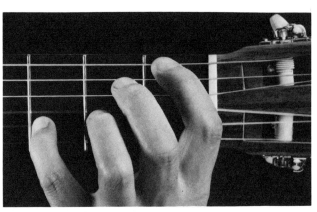

Bar 14 (**f** and **d** notes)

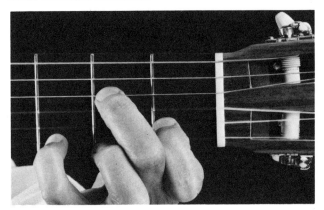

Bar 1 (**e, c** and **g** notes)

Moderato

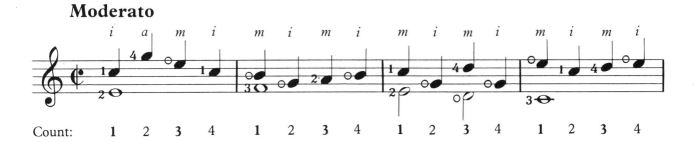

Count: **1** 2 **3** 4   **1** 2 **3** 4   **1** 2 **3** 4   **1** 2 **3** 4

41

The E Major Scale

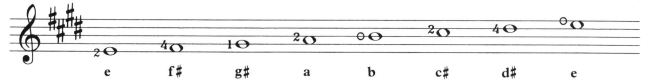

e   f♯   g♯   a   b   c♯   d♯   e

The guitar's 'natural' key, which can involve the first, second and sixth open strings, is the key of E major. The scale in this key has four sharp notes in order to produce the required major scale intervals:

e   f♯   g♯   a   b   c♯   d♯   e

As in the D major and A major pieces, you will sometimes move into the second position with your left hand when playing in the key of E major.

The minor key related to E major is C♯ minor, and like the relative minor keys of D and A major, it is seldom used for guitar music.

Left-Hand Positions

f♯ note

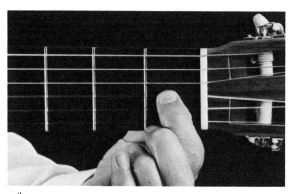

g♯ note

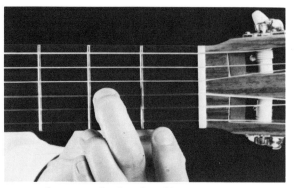

a note (to open 2nd string b)

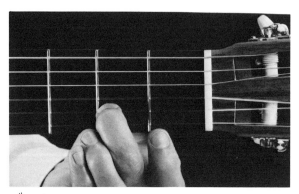

c♯ note

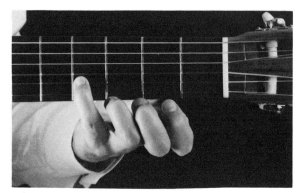

d♯ note (to open 1st string e)

Open Air Russ Shipton

Check on those notes that need to be made sharp: f, c, g, and d. When you're sure of the right frets you should have little trouble playing this piece.

Try to keep your left-hand fingers at right angles to the strings. This is particularly important for clarity in a run like the one in the 7th bar. Economy of left hand movement is essential for smooth playing.

The notes in the lower part will always be played with the right hand thumb, unless otherwise indicated.

Looking at the two last bars of this piece, you can see that they are marked with brackets above the stave and numbered **1.** and **2.** The bar marked **1.** is the first ending. On the repeat you miss the first ending and play the bar marked **2.** This handy device saves writing out the entire piece twice when the only difference in the repeat is one or two final bars.

Slow, stately music of the 16th and 17th centuries was generally written in $\frac{2}{2}$ and $\frac{3}{2}$. The lower 2 means the beats have a time value of a minim, and normally this would mean a more ponderous and deliberate pace. In both $\frac{2}{2}$ and $\frac{3}{2}$, each minim beat requires a stress.

Pavane I Luis Milan

Luis Milan (1500-1561) wrote a number of pavanes (a pavane was a stately dance originating in the 16th century). Though I have considerably shortened these two pieces and used simplified fingering, you'll still be able to appreciate the style.

The positions for the half and full barrés are shown below. In the 12th bar, don't take your first finger off completely – hold the bass f note and the middle a note and let them ring on under the treble note sequence.

Notice the tied c note – (bars 13 and 14) keep the first finger down while the others change.

Try to play these pieces very smoothly, and bring out the full value of each note, stressing each minim beat.

Left-Hand Positions

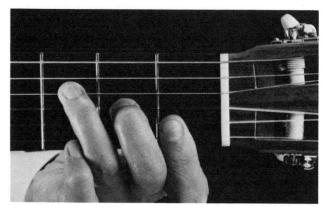

Bar 2 (half-barré)

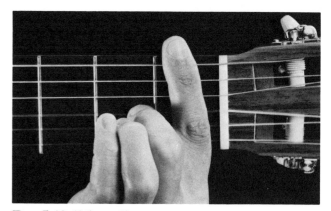

Bar 5 (full-barré)

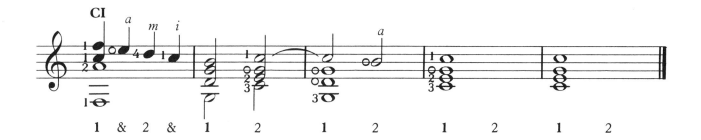

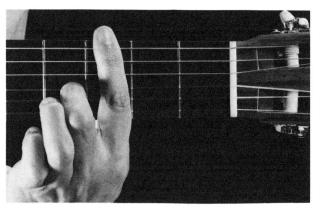

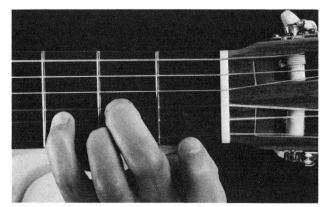

Pavane II Luis Milan

Notice the natural **c** in the 6th bar and the tied **d** notes in the 7th.

The dotted semibreve is equal to three minims in length – in the 3/2 time signature, this means one full bar. Remember to stress each minim beat.

The **d** note in the 4th bar is created by the lift hand (4th finger) using the ligado technique.

Left-Hand Positions

Bar 1 (full barré)

Bar 1 (a, d and f♯ notes)

Maestoso

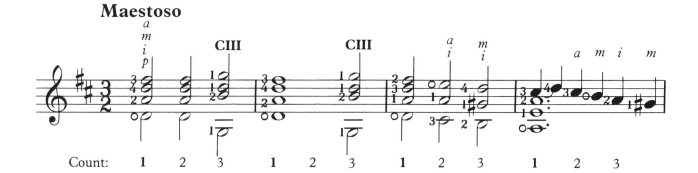

Count: 1   2   3   1   2   3   1   2   3   1   2   3

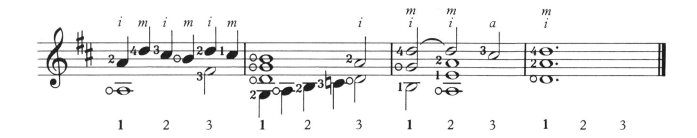

1   2   3   1   2   3   1   2   3   1   2   3

A "3" is sometimes written above or below a group of three notes. This indicates a triplet – three notes played in the time of two of the same value. Thus, when three crotchets are written as ♩♩♩ they will be played in the time normally taken to play two crotchets.

The following piece consists entirely of quavers grouped in triplets. Each note within the triplet carries *exactly* one third of the total value of the beat. They should be counted...
1 & & 2 & & 3 & & etc (If you have any difficulty, you could try saying 'tri – pa – let' to yourself).

Of course, the piece could have been written in $\frac{12}{8}$, which, with its four groups of three quavers, would give exactly the same effect as four sets of triplets in a $\frac{4}{4}$ bar.

Common Triplets Russ Shipton

The right hand pattern for the whole piece is straightforward – thumb followed by index and middle fingers.

Then the 2nd, 3rd and 4th fingers change to the position shown in the third photograph – the 1st finger remains on the f♯ note as an anchor. By moving just the 1st & 2nd fingers you can then change to the position shown in the final photograph – the 3rd & 4th fingers stay where they are.

Remember that the sharp accidental applies to other notes of the same pitch in the same bar.

Quaver triplets are played throughout.
Legato means the notes should be smoothly connected.

Left-Hand Positions

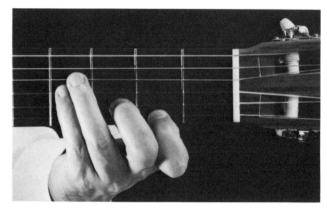

Bar 9

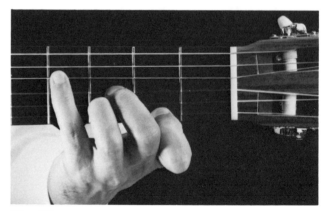

Bar 10

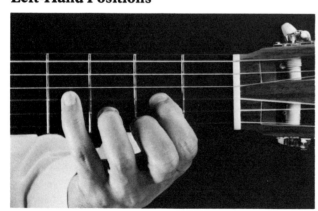

Bar 1

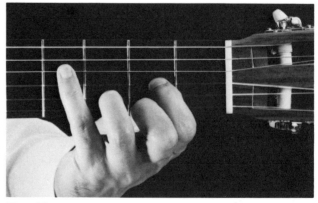

Bar 11

Another beautiful melody from Giuliani gives you the opportunity to examine the $\frac{6}{8}$ rhythm again. One bar of $\frac{6}{8}$ will almost always be divided into two halves of three beats, with stresses on the first and fourth beats of the bar. This can often produce a similar effect to pieces written in $\frac{3}{8}$. The difference between $\frac{3}{8}$ and $\frac{6}{8}$ is that the second stress in a $\frac{6}{8}$ bar is not as strong as the first, whereas each stress (on the first beat of each bar) in $\frac{3}{8}$ is roughly equal, as in the second piece on the next page.

Study Mauro Giuliani

In this piece the treble notes should ring out while the bass part flows gently underneath.

Rallentando means you should slow down a little at that point – use your own judgement as to how much and for how long.

Left-Hand Positions

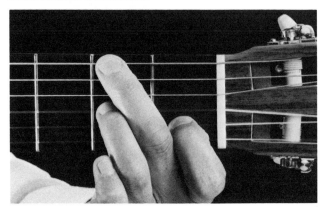

Bar 7

Village Waltz Russ Shipton

The first section is straightforward, but the second section includes semi-quavers and dotted quavers. A dotted quaver has a time value of three semi-quavers. Follow the count carefully and play the next note on the half-beat.

Left-Hand Positions

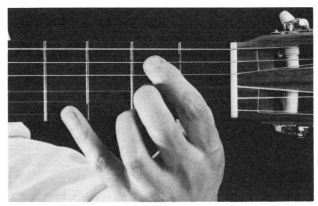

Bar 7

The $\frac{6}{8}$ and $\frac{2}{4}$ time signatures both involve two main pulses per bar. In $\frac{6}{8}$, the overall feel is **123, 223**, while in $\frac{2}{4}$ it is **1, 2**, or **1& , 2&**.
However, if triplets are used for variety in a $\frac{2}{4}$ piece, this can give the effect of a $\frac{6}{8}$ time signature (as in the last section of 'The Duke's March' on the next page).

Bush Jig Russ Shipton

Jigs are for dancing to and are therefore jaunty pieces. 'In Bush Jig', I've included some more **ligado** practice – the triplet in the 4th bar is played on the third beat, so count 1 2 3 & & for the half bar. Hammer your finger on and pull off again quickly.

Don't be frightened of striking the bass notes firmly, especially for this piece.

Notice the dotted crotchet rest in the bass part of the 4th bar – dotted rests work the same way as dotted notes, the dot increasing the length by half as much again. Pause slightly on the **fermata** in the 8th bar, and don't miss the accidentals resulting from the brief key change.

Vivace means fast and lively.

Left-Hand Positions

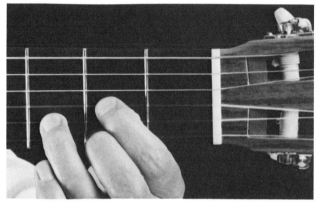

Bar 1

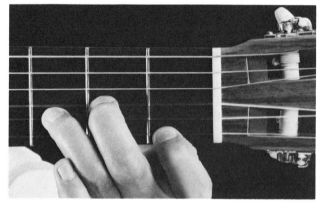

Bar 5

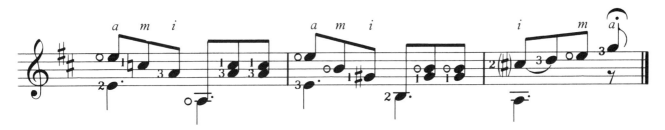

The Duke's March Russ Shipton

Count the second section carefully, and try to keep the overall tempo of the piece constant. Apart from remembering the three sharps, the fingering is simple.

The F Major Scale

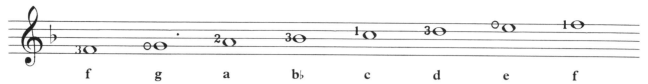

f   g   a   b♭   c   d   e   f

F major is not a very popular key for guitar music. In fact flat keys are generally avoided in guitar composition. But here are two short and melodic pieces in F major and its relative, D minor. The expected notes will be those of the F major scale, where only one note needs to be altered:

f g a b♭ c d e f

Thus the key signature for F major and D minor is one flat: B. You'll notice in the Bourreé on page 54 that the c note is made sharp. As we've seen before, the usual practice in minor keys is to sharpen the note before the tonic, the seventh degree of the scale.

Left-Hand Positions

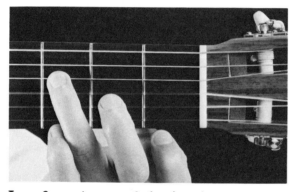

Low f note (to open 3rd string **g**)

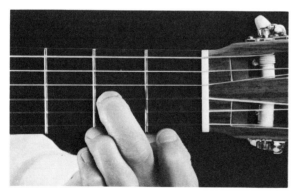

a note

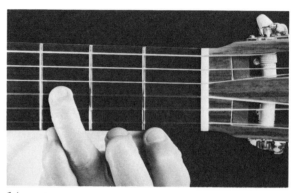

b♭ note

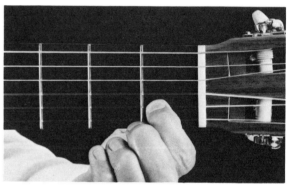

c note

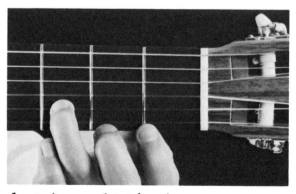

d note (to open 1st string **e**)

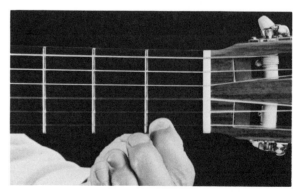

High f note

Minuet in F Antonio Diabelli

Use your right-hand thumb for just the first beat in bars 2, 4, & 6.

Left hand positions are held for one bar each. The first two positions and the half barré are shown in the photographs. Move your 1st finger to the bass f note just when you need to play it for the close of the piece.

Left-Hand Positions

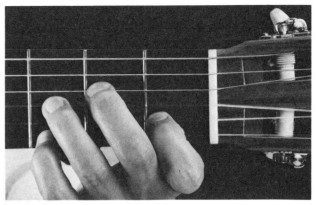

Bar 2

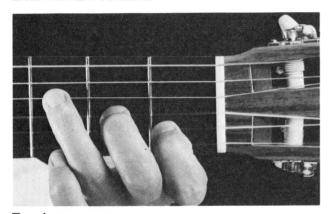

Bar 1

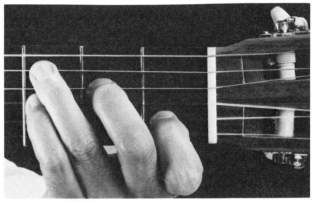

Bar 3

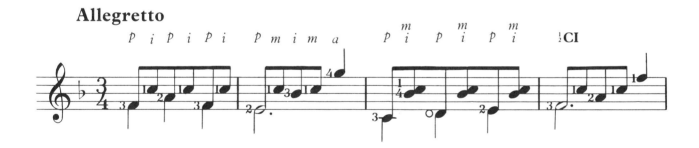

Bourrée <small>Robert De Visée</small>

Robert De Visée (1650-1722) was a guitarist and lutenist in the Court of Louis XIV of France.

Work through the left hand fingering, bar by bar. It's a little complicated, but not too difficult. Slide the little finger up when moving to the 2nd bar. In the 3rd bar, the 3rd finger goes from the c♯ to the d on the second string because the little finger is then needed for the g on the first string.

In the 4th bar, the 3rd finger again moves from the c♯ to the d for ease of fingering.

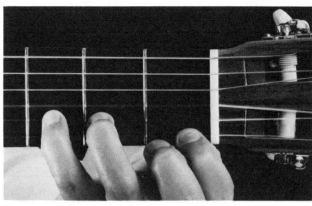

Bar 4

Left-Hand Positions

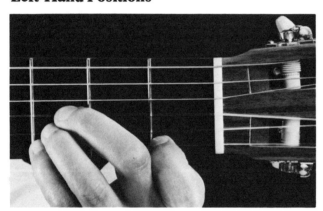

Bar 2

Apoyando

The **apoyando,** or rest stroke, is for greater emphasis and volume. Strike the third string with the index finger and come to rest on the fourth string. Keep the finger quite firm and straight as you strike. Then use your thumb to strike the sixth string, and come to rest on the fifth string.

Single note passages, perhaps as the higher part of a duet, may often be played using rest strokes. This technique will produce clear and accurate melody lines. Where the bass and treble parts are both played by a single guitar, free strokes are generally used. But, where particular parts of the melody need to be accented, or the melody notes of an arpeggio style accompaniment need to be differentiated from the others, rest strokes can be used for greater volume.

Occasionally, the right hand thumb may use the rest stroke to emphasise a bass run, but rest strokes are mostly used for melody notes, which are usually in the treble part.

Thumb strikes

After striking

Finger strikes

After striking

55

Minuet Johann Sebastian Bach

Johann Sebastian Bach (1685-1750) was the greatest and most prolific of the Bach family of composers. His work covers many mediums – notably the harpsichord, from which this famous minuet has been adapted.

The minuet was a French court dance in the 17th century. It should be stately, but played at a medium pace once you've mastered the varied left-hand fingering. Check each bar carefully before proceeding because different fingers are often required for the same notes. Two positions are shown to help you. Make sure you hold the bass notes and let them ring as long as written.

The right hand finger indications are not meant to be rigid. Make any changes that help to make your playing smoother.

Use rest strokes for the first treble note of each bar, and then try rest strokes for all of the treble notes.

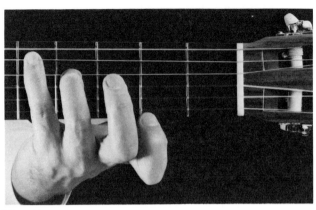

Bar 7

Left-Hand Positions

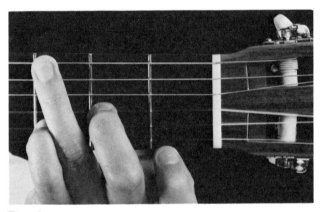

Bar 1

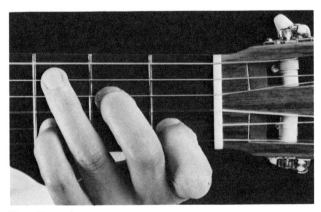

Bar 3

Andantino

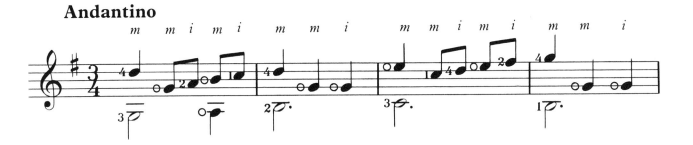

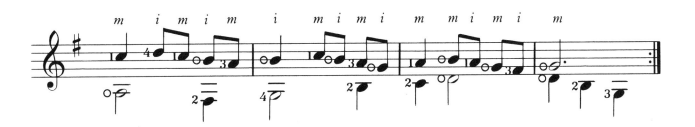

So far you've learnt a variety of pieces which have involved notes on the first four frets plus the a note at the 5th fret of the first string. These last few pages contain several well-known melodies that include notes further up the fingerboard. The fingering isn't difficult, and some positions are shown in photos to help you. If you take each position and bar at a time you'll progress quickly. Take the tempo very slowly at first.

Greensleeves Anon. (Attrib. to Henry VIII)

This pretty tune has been popular for 400 years! You should be able to follow the melody notes up the fingerboard easily enough. Check the top line first for melody and rhythm; then follow the fingering for the accompaniment bar by bar. The two shapes played in the 5th position are shown below – the rest of the left hand fingering is straightforward.

The right hand fingering is also straightforward, apart from the fast **arpeggiando** across the chords (those with this sign: ↕). Start playing the bass note with your thumb **just** before the beat, and play the three treble notes one after the other, quickly. The last note must be played as the beat finishes. In other words, instead of playing the notes at the same time, as a chord, they are played very quickly, from bass to treble. This gives the piece a more stately and mediaeval sound.

Follow the count carefully for the dotted quaver with semi-quaver. Sometimes these are replaced by equal quavers or (as in the 3rd bar from the end) by a crotchet and two semi-quavers.

Bar 2

Bar 18

Left-Hand Positions

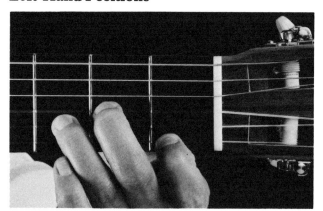

Bar 1

Spanish Ballad (Romanza) Anon.

This beautiful melody is perhaps the most popular of all classical guitar pieces. The first section (shown here) involves a full barré and a long stretch for the left hand, but is otherwise straightforward. Open strings are used in most bars to harmonize the high melody notes.

Once you have located all of the notes and have mastered the fingering, you can build up some speed. Remember that the melody is carried by the first note of each triplet. You can make these notes ring out by playing them all with rest strokes. A technique called **vibrato** may be used to add expression and feeling to these melody notes. Vibrato is achieved by fretting the note securely and then moving the left hand so that the finger 'rolls' back and forth slightly (in line with the string).

Left-Hand Positions

Bar 1 (**high b** with open strings)

Bar 5 (**high e** with open strings)

Bar 7 (**half barré**)

Bar 9 (**full barré,** then add **c** note)

Bar 10 (**full barré,** then add **d♯**)

Bourrée Johann Sebastian Bach

This second Bach masterpiece is excellent practice for left and right hand agility and co-ordination, as well as being a very enjoyable piece to play.

Learn it bar by bar and practise each left hand manoeuvre separately at first. Then put the bars together, slowly at first.

Hold your left hand fingers quite near the strings all the time because the movements are frequent and rapid.

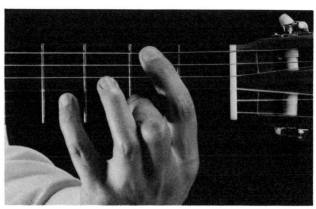

Bar 2 (**f♯** and **c♯** notes, to **d♯**)

Left-Hand Positions

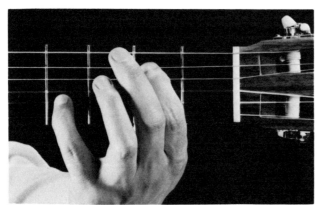

Bar 1 (**b** and **d♯** notes)

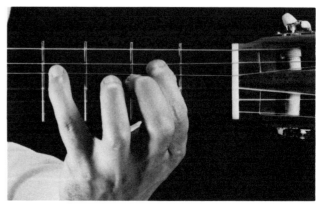

Bar 4 (**b** and **g** notes, to **f♯**)

Scarborough Fair Traditional

You'll notice that three parts instead of two are shown. The top part is the melody, which you should examine first. The bottom part is mainly an e drone, while the middle part provides the harmonic and rhythmic filling.

Written music can never show *exactly* how a guitar piece should sound, because some notes ring on and others don't. Thus, a compromise is reached whereby the composer's main intentions

are shown and the music is straightforward to follow.

Like Romanza, this arrangement involves open string accompaniment in most bars. The diamond-shaped notes at the end are known as **harmonics.** To play them, place a left hand finger over the first three strings at the 12th fret, directly over the 12th fret **wire** (just touching the strings). Pluck with the right hand and remove the left hand finger quickly.

Closing comments

Congratulations! You're now able to read and play various classical music styles. You have the basis to go on to more difficult music by the famous names in this book or classical guitar music by modern composers.

Below I've listed several collections of classical pieces and arrangements you might like to try:

Classical Guitar Collection, Volume 1 Edited Harvey Vinson
Classical Guitar Collection, Volume 2 Edited Harvey Vinson
Classical Guitar Collection, Volume 3 Edited Leonid Bolotine
The Beatles For Classical Guitar Arranged Joe Washington
The Baroque Guitar Selected and edited by Frederick Noad
The Classical Guitar Selected and edited by Frederick Noad
The Renaissance Guitar Selected and edited by Frederick Noad
The Guitar Songbook Selected and edited by Frederick Noad
Folksingers Guide to Classical Guitar by Harvey Vinson
Fingerpicking Bach by Marcel Robinson

All titles published by Music Sales Limited, 8/9 Frith Street, London W1V 5TZ, England

6/95 (26362)